Wet and Dry

Kelly Doudna

Published by SandCastle™, an imprint of ABDO Publishing Company, 4940 Viking Drive, Edina, Minnesota 55435.

Printed in the United States.

Photo credits: Artville, Corel, Photodisc.

Library of Congress Cataloging-in-Publication Data

Doudna, Kelly, 1963-
    Wet and Dry / Kelly Doudna.
      p. cm. -- (Opposites)
    Summary: Simple rhymes point out the difference between wet and dry.
    ISBN 1-57765-149-9 (alk. paper) -- ISBN 1-57765-282-7 (set)
    3. English language--Synonyms and antonyms--Juvenile literature. 2. Readers (Primary) [1. Readers. 2. English language--Synonyms and antonyms.] I. Title.

PE1591 D66 2000
428.1--dc21

99-046486

The SandCastle concept, content, and reading method have been reviewed and approved by a national advisory board including literacy specialists, librarians, elementary school teachers, early childhood education professionals, and parents.

Let Us Know

After reading the book, SandCastle would like you to tell us your stories about reading. What is your favorite page? Was there something hard that you needed help with? Share the ups and downs of learning to read. We want to hear from you! To get posted on the Abdo Publishing Company Web site, send us email at:

sandcastle@abdopub.com

About SandCastle™

Nonfiction books for the beginning reader

- Basic concepts of phonics are incorporated with integrated language methods of reading instruction. Most words are short, and phrases, letter sounds, and word sounds are repeated.

- Readability is determined by the number of words in each sentence, the number of characters in each word, and word lists based on curriculum frameworks.

- Full-color photography reinforces word meanings and concepts.

- "Words I Can Read" list at the end of each book teaches basic elements of grammar, helps the reader recognize the words in the text, and builds vocabulary.

- Reading levels are indicated by the number of flags on the castle.

Look for more SandCastle books in these three reading levels:

Level 1 (one flag)	Level 2 (two flags)	Level 3 (three flags)
Grades Pre-K to K 5 or fewer words per page	**Grades K to 1** 5 to 10 words per page	**Grades 1 to 2** 10 to 15 words per page

Land is **dry**.

My turtle crawls past.

The ocean is **wet**.

Two yellow fish swim fast.

Cookies are **dry**.

I have not finished mine yet.

I like milk.

Anything I can drink is **wet**.

This flower is **dry**.

It is in the sun.

This flower is **wet**.

Count the raindrops just for fun.

We are **wet**.

We play in the spray.

My big towel will **dry** the water away.

What do you see that is **wet** or **dry**?

Words I Can Read

Nouns

A noun is a person, place, or thing

flower (FLOW-ur) pp. 13, 15
fun (FUHN) p. 15
land (LAND) p. 5
milk (MILK) p. 11
ocean (OH-shuhn) p. 7
spray (SPRAY) p. 17
sun (SUHN) p. 13
towel (TOW-uhl) p. 19
turtle (TUR-tuhl) p. 5
water (WAW-tur) p. 19

Plural Nouns

A plural noun is more than one
person, place, or thing

cookies (KUK-eez) p. 9
fish (FISH) p. 7
raindrops (RAYN-dropss) p. 15

Verbs

A verb is an action or being word

are (AR) pp. 9, 17
can (KAN) p. 11

22

count (KOWNT) p. 15
crawls (KRAWLZ) p. 5
do (DOO) p. 21
drink (DRINGK) p. 11
dry (DRYE) p. 19
finished (FIN-isht) p. 9
have (HAV) p. 9
is (IZ) pp. 5, 7, 11, 13, 15, 21
like (LIKE) p. 11
play (PLAY) p. 17
see (SEE) p. 21
swim (SWIM) p. 7
will (WIL) p. 19

Adjectives

An adjective describes something

big (BIG) p. 19
dry (DRYE) pp. 5, 9, 13, 21
mine (MINE) p. 9
my (MYE) pp. 5, 19
this (THISS) pp. 13, 15
two (TOO) p. 7
wet (WET) pp. 7, 11, 15, 17, 21
yellow (YEL-oh) p. 7

Picture Words

ocean

towel

spray

turtle

Word Families

Words that have the same vowel
and ending letters

-ast	**-un**
fast	fun
past	sun
-et	**-ay**
wet	away
yet	spray